writing action

A Book of Writing Prompts

the san francisco writers' grotto

authors of *642 Things to Write About*

foreword by Bonnie Tsui

ABRAMS NOTERIE, NEW YORK

writing action

You're sitting at your desk, attempting to write about a hair-raising road trip that nearly derailed your whole life. Your pen hovers above the paper; you can *feel* the adrenaline firing up your brain. But this is the only sentence you manage to eke out: *We were driving on I-5 and suddenly this car came at us out of nowhere, and then I was so scared I thought we were going to . . .*

Already the words fall short of the mark. You were *there*. You saw the car coming the wrong way. You experienced the metallic tang of fear, the jolt of your heart, the strange quiet that descended over you like a blanket. But you can't seem to make your version of events match the reality.

No one said capturing pure, real-time action on the page was easy. Such writing relies on brilliant verb selection and a sense of mystery and timing and—*bang*—a satisfying crescendo.

This opening paragraph from Susan Casey's book *The Devil's Teeth* has just about everything you could want in an action scene:

> The killing took place at dawn and as usual it was a decapita-
> tion, accomplished by a single vicious swipe. Blood geysered
> into the air, creating a vivid slick that stood out on the water
> like the work of a violent abstract painter. Five hundred yards
> away, outside of a lighthouse on the island's highest peak, a

man watched through a telescope. First he noticed the frenzy
of gulls, bird gestalt that signaled trouble. And then he saw the
blood. Grabbing his radio, he turned and began to run.

Blood and *geyser* aren't often found in the same sentence.
But Casey puts them together here and suddenly we're
checking our own bodies for cuts. Also note the mystery:
Who died, and who is this man watching through the
telescope? A voyeur? A co-conspirator? Is he running *from*
or *to* the geyser of blood? These are excellent questions,
arising from the tension she creates. We want to turn the
page to find out what happens next—and with action that's
always the reaction you're after.

Back to the exciting road trip you're struggling to describe:
After you've written and scratched out that first sentence
a few times, try a new tack. In the prompts section of this
book, you'll find two "road trip" exercises. The first (on page
16) is to write a draft of your story. The second (on page 18)
is a multistep prompt: First, write down all the verbs you can
think of that are related to the event. Second, write down all
the nouns. Then think about all the hyperbolic feelings and
ideas that bubble up when you go over the event again and
again, and write down adjectives to describe that hyperbole.
When you're done, you should have a brainstorm sheet that
makes you smile or laugh or even cry. It should bring back
vivid memories, and there should be some pretty ludicrous
words on the paper, words that you may not use very often. If
you're not seeing words like that, keep adding to the sheet. *Is,
were, going, drive, it, car, man, kid, bicycle, tree, loud, sad, hot,*

black, *silly*, *smoky*, *bored*—your brainstorm sheet should not be trafficking in words like these. You want words like *hurtled*, *exploded*, *ransacked*, *bulldozed*, *careening*, *monster*, *freight*, *wasp*, *stupor*, *slice*, *eardrum*, *unjust*, *crushing*, *animalistic*, *acrid*, *twisting*, *wine-dark*, et cetera. You want words that provoke.

When you're done, try that first sentence of your road-trip story again.

For further inspiration, let's look at what happens next in that murderous excerpt from Casey's book, a few paragraphs on in the narrative:

> Peter unhooked the winch, an inch-thick cable of steel, as the whaler rose and fell into troughs big enough to swallow it. He started the engine and powered two hundred yards toward the birds, where the object of all the attention floated in a cloud of blood: a quarter-ton elephant seal was missing its head. The odor was dense and oily, rancid Crisco mixed with seawater.
>
> "Oh yeah," Peter said, "That's the smell of a shark attack."

So much is revealed here through precise word choices that support the action. We learn about the victim and the killer. We get energetic verbs, and we get evocative sights and smells that bind it all together. Casey could have stopped with "troughs" when describing the chop of the water, but she adds that they are "big enough to swallow" a whaler. She could have stopped with "dense and oily" to describe the smell, but she adds "rancid Crisco mixed with seawater." Details like these, so precise we can feel them on our skin and up our noses, move us just as much as verbs do. These paragraphs yank us headlong into the world of Peter ("the man" in the first paragraph, a scientist stationed in the Farallon Islands near San Francisco). They create momentum that carries us—no, *blasts* us; note the improved verb choice!—into the heart of the book.

Let's say your road-trip story wasn't all that action-packed; perhaps it was more about the intense rumination and epiphany that followed a brief, catalyzing, near-death moment. You're after an action-floating-in-a-sea-of-thoughts kind of scene. This requires a slightly different approach. I recently found myself trying to integrate this sort of action into a scene for a book I'm writing. Here's how it turned out:

Jay Taylor had been in Iraq just three days when he woke up and found his friend J. P. Santana's prosthetic arm on his doorstep. A second before, Taylor had been juggling his first load of Baghdad-washed laundry, depositing it in his FEMA trailer, just inside the complex that housed the embassy staff.

Then came the mortar blast. It threw Taylor against a wall and knocked him into a daze. It blew Santana—who'd come by to collect Taylor for dinner—thirty feet down the road, minus his arm. Santana yelled back to Taylor, "Let me hear your voice! I'm OK! Are you OK?" Taylor shouted in the affirmative. Santana's own trailer was obliterated. A man across the street was killed.

If Santana had been a little bit later to Taylor's door, "if he'd decided to shower," Taylor says, "he would have been dead."

Amid the dust and debris, Santana retrieved his prosthetic arm, and Special Forces quickly arrived to seal off the trailer of the man who'd been killed. Santana's trailer, still smoldering, was cordoned off. The troops told Santana and Taylor to come back in an hour. With nothing else to do but wait, the two men headed to dinner at the cavernous mess hall. Outside the door was an oil drum full of sand, into which armed personnel were required to discharge their weapons—*click click*—to show that they weren't loaded.

"The odd thing is, even the first time being in a bombing situation like that, we just get up and say, 'Oh, I hope they still have meatloaf,'" Taylor tells me, shaking his head.

Taylor and Santana are big characters in my book. It's a work of journalism, so I'm responsible for reporting the truth of the events I'm talking about, but that truth is complex. I don't want to just recount an explosion. I want to recount what was going on in the characters' heads, too. Yes, there is action-packed drama in this scene—an actual explosion—but just as crucially there is the mundane aftermath, the coping-by-eating. I chose to mix a bit of *real-time action* (that precise dramatic moment, unfolding as it happens) with *narrative summary* (the compressed, explanatory sum-up of what happened afterward); the latter slows the action down and gives us time to digest the meaning behind it. This extra time allows me to underscore the peculiar logic to life in a place where you are in constant danger of being blown up.

A feeling of urgency, but with some depth: That's what real-time action mixed with narrative summary can get you.

You say your road-trip action was even *more* mundane than a coping meal of meatloaf in a war zone? That what you're trying to capture is catharsis more than blood-pumping action? Well, such scenes can certainly be composed of small but telling actions that together signal something momentous. Consider this micro-scene from Zadie Smith's novel *White Teeth*:

> Later that morning, Archie did an ecstatic eight circuits of Swiss Cottage traffic in his car, his head stuck out the window, a stream of air hitting the teeth at the back of his mouth like a windsock . . . laughing like a loon.

Most of us are like Archie. Workaday characters who, on those rare, remarkable days, experience something extraordinary or, at least, *feel* something extraordinary that must be revealed. We're not watching elephant-seal decapitations or fleeing aerial bombings. Like Archie, we spend a lot of time driving around the neighborhood, and sometimes it's a truly liberating part of our day. That sort of mundane action matters, too. For most of us, it matters the *most*. We have to capture it with the specificity of a blood-geysering event, or we risk losing our audience.

Smith runs no risk of losing us in Archie's mundane ride. She makes it clear that this is no ordinary loop around the hood. This is "ecstatic" time; Archie's head out the window resembles that of an overexcited puppy. Archie laughs the maniacal laugh of a man who has just gotten a new lease on life. *Something is up, people*, Smith tells us (without actually telling us), and we turn the page to find out what that is.

But maybe your road-trip action isn't *really* about you so much as it is about something beyond your understanding, an ineffable thing that changed everything as it flung itself in your path. What then? Well, as Lauren Groff reveals in her short story "The Midnight Zone," sometimes the action occurring outside of you is a pretty good match for the churning internal feeling you're after. You can use that external action to evoke feeling better than a scream or a description of physical upset ever could:

> It rubbed itself against the little cabin and played at the corners and broke sticks off the trees and tossed them at the roof so they jigged down like creatures with strange and scrabbling claws.

This is the wind as the grim reaper, as a restless, disquieting feeling that permeates the page. We are scared on behalf of the characters caught in this wind. We do not need to hear the characters in this story say they are scared. The wind, its actions minutely described, tells us. Just this small shift, to a new point of view, gives the page a new pulse and readers a new reason to keep turning.

Consider the possibilities of this approach as you sit down to write your road-trip action. Out-of-control weather, erratic birds, the low moan of a long-haul truck horn—these can be proxies for the feeling your action scene wants to stir up. They can reveal, without your characters having to utter a word. Let's take another look inside your car. Which of the following is more effective in conveying your internal freak-out?

a) ". . . then I was so scared."

b) ". . . then the wind hurled itself against the windshield and tore sticks off the trees and tossed them at the glass."

Time to return to your three-part brainstorm exercise. If the page is swimming with words, you're ready. Before you restart your action scene, though, ask yourself what kind of action you want it to be: pure, real-time action; a mix of real-time action and narrative summary; something more physically mundane but emotionally ecstatic; or a passage girded by mood and the mystifying actions of forces beyond your grasp? These four are not the only kinds of action scenes out there, but they're a solid starter set. And if you know which one you'd prefer to experiment with, then you can pluck the exact words from your list that will convey the drama you're after.

Writing, by the way, is action. So the minute your pen hits the paper, you're on your way.

. . . .

BONNIE TSUI is a longtime contributor to the *New York Times* and the author of the award-winning *American Chinatown*. She has written about big-wave surfers, Hong Kong rooftop farmers, Michelin street food, kid break-dancers, wildfires, and more for *California Sunday*, the *New York Times Magazine*, and *The New Yorker* online. Her next book, *Why We Swim*, will be published by Algonquin Books in 2020. Find her on Twitter @bonnietsui.

writing action: a summary

- **Verb selection is key.** Choose verbs that are specific and impactful and that best convey the emotional tenor of the scene. This applies to word choice in general.

- **Timing is everything.** Strike a balance between describing action in *real time* (writing an account of events as they unfold) and *narrative summary* (such as shifting to a particular character's point of view, introducing a flashback, or summarizing and compressing to move the narrative forward).

- **Build in mystery.** As the actions in your story take place, hold back some detail. Some sentences should raise questions that propel your reader to keep looking for answers.

- **Engage the senses.** Make your readers feel as if they are physically part of the action. What sights, sounds, scents, and other sensations are they experiencing?

- **Small actions, big results.** Any activity can be infused with emotion. A quotidian task, depending on how it is performed, can build suspense or add depth to the character.

- **Animate the inanimate.** Any setting (or the objects within that setting) can be supercharged with action and emotion to help convey the feelings of a character.

writing prompts

Pick up a favorite book or magazine
and circle every verb and turn of phrase
that impresses you. List them here.

words to remember

the road trip to end all road trips

Write down a brief first draft of a recent road trip, from your perspective.

improve the road-trip language

List some nouns you used in your first draft of the road trip in
the previous exercise.

_____

_____

_____

_____

_____

Jot down more vivid noun choices here.

_____

_____

_____

_____

_____

List the verbs you used in your first draft of the road trip.

_____

_____

_____

_____

_____

_____

Now write down more provocative verb choices here.

_____

_____

_____

_____

_____

List any use of figurative language or hyperbole in your first
draft. If you didn't use any, what could you enhance while still
remaining truthful?

_____

_____

_____

_____

_____

Rewrite the first sentence of your road trip here, using new
nouns, verbs, and figurative language.

_____

_____

_____

_____

_____

road trip revisited

Write a brief account of your recent road trip from another passenger's perspective.

an imaginative leap

Of course you can't really know what the other passengers experienced, but try to put yourself in their shoes, see the events from their seats, and consider their fears and expectations of the trip. They are not the same as yours.

plain becomes specific

One of the best ways to strengthen action scenes is to find more specific ways to say something plain. "He picked up the baby" becomes "The baby was cotton candy in his hands, sweet but almost too delicate to touch." Write three plain sentences about a simple act (brushing teeth, climbing into bed, etc.), then rewrite them for specificity.

engage your senses

List five smells in your office or the room you are currently in.

_____

_____

_____

_____

_____

Describe how one of those smells got there.

_____

_____

_____

_____

_____

List five sounds from this room.

_____

_____

_____

_____

_____

_____

Animate one of the sounds. Give it temperament to stand in
for how you're feeling.

_____

_____

_____

_____

_____

Look around. Is there a window nearby? What can you see
from it?

_____

_____

_____

_____

_____

What would someone looking into your window (or doorway)
see of you?

_____

_____

_____

_____

_____

learn from the best

Copy an action-filled passage (preferably one in which the events are described in real-time, as they unfold) from a favorite book or article.

power words

- Notice the verbs and circle your favorites.

- Notice where the mystery resides; circle it.

- Rewrite one of the best sentences from the excerpt, even though it may seem impossible to improve.

List five objects in your kitchen from least menacing to most. Animate the chosen kitchen objects by putting each one into a sentence; give each a specific emotion.

kitchen detail

what's cooking?

Watch someone prepare a meal and describe the process.

Now rewrite the cooking description to telegraph sadness in the cook's actions, maybe giving a kitchen appliance temperament to stand in for the cook's.

a physical exercise

Describe a bear on the attack. To get closer to the words you're after, imitate the motion of the bear with your own body.

live! sports! commentary!

Watch a TV clip of a brief sporting event—a hundred-meter dash or a twenty-five-meter freestyle sprint. Write a page narrating the action.

adding more color

- Write from the perspective of the finish-line tape.

- Give the weather a mood.

- Describe one runner's leg muscles in minute detail.

shift the perspective

Write a short scene about someone arriving at a high school reunion and what this person observes upon entering the room.

Try your hand at the same scene, but replace the primary character with someone else in the scene. How does the replacement affect everything that occurs?

sob stories

Describe someone crying, trying three different approaches.
Describe not just the face but the whole body and the
character's gaze.

no voices

Visit a zoo or playground and observe an interaction between two young children. Without using dialogue, write a paragraph that focuses on action to relay how they communicate with each other.

left unspoken

Is one child the leader and the other the follower? Are they comfortable together? Is there a moment when the dynamic changes?

nothing really happened

Write a paragraph about a mundane activity, using descriptive, detailed language to urge the reader on. Think about the emotion behind the small scene that can help animate it and give it some urgency.

ordinary tasks

- Making photocopies at the last minute before a meeting

- Doing Sunday-morning tasks—making coffee, going grocery shopping—after an amazing Saturday-night date

- Unpacking after a terrible vacation

the daily grind

Find the ecstatic in the everyday. Start by listing the customs of a typical day.

Now go back and rewrite each custom as an *event*,
a harbinger of exceptional things to come.

amp up the little things

Imagine a library full of people, and describe one person's behavior in a way that makes his or her small and quiet actions exciting.

winners vs. losers

Describe the most competitive game of hopscotch ever from the point of view of one of the competitors—the person winning.

Now write the hopscotch scene from the point of view of the other competitor—the person coming in second place.

_____

_____

_____

_____

_____

_____

_____

_____

_____

_____

_____

_____

_____

_____

_____

_____

_____

_____

playing with time

Your plane hits terrible turbulence. Describe your reaction, the reactions of fellow passengers, and the physical sensations of the plane as a real-time action scene—with the immediate events unfolding as you tell them.

Now try rewriting the same scene using elements of narrative summary, by deepening the context and capturing events over a longer period of time.

_____

_____

_____

_____

_____

_____

_____

_____

_____

_____

_____   **narrative summary**

_____   Try using flashback
                                                          (recounting what a
_____   passenger was doing at
                                                          the gate prior to board-
_____   ing, for example, or
                                                          what another passenger
_____   was doing at home that
                                                          morning), or describe
_____   what different characters
                                                          were thinking. You can
_____   use dialogue or even skip
                                                          ahead in time.
_____

casing the joint

Follow a little girl as she walks through an animal shelter,
looking to adopt.

Describe a shoplifter casing the perfume aisle at a store and then stealing an item.

escalating events

You are coming home and see three men having a heated
argument in front of your apartment building. You can tell
that their conflict is escalating, even before you're within
earshot. Describe their actions.

Coincidentally, just as you reach the entrance of your building a police car pulls up. The men think that you called the cops. Describe what happens next.

think fast

Two people are on a train platform. Person A passes out.
Person B doesn't know CPR. What does Person B do?

timing is everything

Try to combine real-time action (the stuff happening on the train platform) with events in the past, in summary. For instance, what if Person B, in order to cope with what is going on, narrates a memory from her simple morning—the cereal she ate before leaving for the train, the section of the newspaper she perused— and how it made her feel.

the accidental grocery heist

You're at the grocery checkout counter. You've forgotten your wallet, but you need to leave with your items. Get out.

what if?

You're jolted awake by a 7.0 magnitude earthquake. Use all your senses to describe the scene, touching on sights, sounds, and smells, as well as the character of the shaking.

make me a drink

Observe a bartender serving a customer at the bar. Jot down the details of their physical movements and body language, and give the drink your attention too.

Now use your observations to write a scene imagining a prior
relationship between the bartender and customer.

in the driver's seat

Describe a (terrified) teenage student's first driving lesson.

Describe a (reckless and overconfident) teenage student's first driving lesson.

getting swaggy

Describe a sixteen-year-old boy picking out clothes and dressing for a date.

finding the exit

You're in a room full of balloons and can't find the exit, which wouldn't scare most people, but you're terrified of balloons. Write about how you make it out of the room (or don't).

the last orange on earth

Peel an orange. Observe it using all your senses—smell it, taste it, touch it, listen in. Write out the experience.

Drop a ball, a pan, a book, a belt, and an assortment of other objects on the floor. List the sounds they make and describe how they make you feel.

sound and fury

loch ness?

You walk to the end of a diving board, look down, and see something strange at the bottom of the pool. Build suspense and mystery as you describe the scene.

building suspense

Don't give it all away in the first sentence. Reread the examples by Susan Casey in the opening essay of this book (pages 3 through 5). Start with minutely observed details, then add in curious actions that might not make sense at first blush but are nevertheless crystal clear, then end with a high-speed finale in which all is revealed.

do I know you?

As you hear the taxi doors lock, you realize the driver looks familiar. Describe the process of figuring out how you know each other and what happens when you are dropped off.

unspeakable

Your characters are playing charades. Have one character act out to another something too painful to say (see sidebar for ideas).

say it isn't so

- He wants to end the relationship.

- She lost her wedding ring.

- He got an F in PE.

- The bank account is empty.

- She's being sent overseas.

you can't hide

Find an antagonistic conversation from the Internet
(Twitter or Facebook comments are often sources of this).
Copy it down.

Rewrite this excerpt as an emotional action scene in which the two opposing commenters are meeting face-to-face.

dawning realities

You are stuffing your clothes into a dryer at a laundromat
when you notice a man with a shotgun sipping coffee nearby.
Describe this scene, escalating the tension.

a gradual shift

Move from the seemingly dull details of laundry (the drudgery!) to your increasingly panicked focus on the armed man and his behavior.

security line

Imagine you are waiting at a security checkpoint at the airport. Describe a physical exchange between two people at the X-ray machine, and use their movements to indicate the nature and history of their relationship. (Do they pass things to each other intimately, or with reserve?)

your last nerve

You're trapped in an elevator with five people for twenty-four hours. Write about the eighteenth hour, when everyone is asleep except for you and the stranger who is trying to jimmy open the doors.

you should've signaled

Someone you accidentally cut off in traffic is now following you home. Write about the realization and the resulting action.

juggling act

Write a scene in which you're rushing to work, but everything is going wrong: You wake up late; you can't find your keys; you're running for the train. You get there just as the train pulls up to the platform.

As the train pulls up to the platform, you're still across the street, and then your mother calls your cell phone. See how it feels to feather in more and more action.

found and lost

Describe the moment of catching a fly baseball in the stands,
then, in the next moment, having it wrestled from your hands.

the delivery

Open the mailbox. There's one green envelope in the pile. It's what you've been waiting for. Describe how you open the envelope, using actions that express how much this piece of mail means to you.

Designer: Debbie Berne
Project Managers: Meghan Ward and Danielle Svetcov
Art Director: Diane Shaw
Editor: Karrie Witkin
Production Manager: Rebecca Westall

ISBN: 978-1-4197-3830-2

Foreword © 2019 Bonnie Tsui
Text © 2019 The Grotto, LLC
Cover illustration: Sabri Deniz Kizil/Shutterstock
Cover © 2019 Abrams

Special thanks to: Alicia Tan, Alissa Greenberg, Ashley Albert, Audrey Ferber,
Beth Winegarner, Bonnie Tsui, Bridget Quinn, Caroline Paul, Celeste Chan,
Chris Colin, Christopher Cook, Constance Hale, Diana Kapp, Elizabeth Stark,
Frances Stroh, Grace Prasad, Hunter Oatman-Stanford, Jane Ciabattari,
Jaya Padmanabhan, Jenny Bitner, Jesus Sierra, Kathryn Ma, Kristen Cosby,
Laura Fraser, Lindsey Crittenden, Lisa Gray, Lisa Hix, Lisa Lerner, Liza Boyd,
Lyzette Wanzer, Mark Wallace, Mary Ladd, Maury Zeff, Maw Shein Win,
Paul Drexler, Shanthi Sekaran, Stephanie Losee, Thaisa Frank, Todd Oppenheimer,
Vanessa Hua, Yukari Kane, Zahra Noorbakhsh

Printed and bound in China

10 9 8 7 6 5 4 3 2 1

Abrams Noterie products are available at special discounts when purchased
in quantity for premiums and promotions as well as fundraising or educational
use. Special editions can also be created to specification. For details, contact
specialsales@abramsbooks.com or the address below.

Abrams Noterie® is a registered trademark of Harry N. Abrams, Inc.

ABRAMS The Art of Books
195 Broadway, New York, NY 10007
abramsbooks.com